October

by Mari Kesselring
Illustrated by Ronnie Rooney

Content Consultant:
Susan Kesselring, MA
Literacy Educator and Preschool Director

visit us at www.abdopublishing.com

Published by Magic Wagon, a division of the ABDO Group, 8000 West 78th Street, Edina, Minnesota 55439. Copyright © 2010 by Abdo Consulting Group, Inc. International copyrights reserved in all countries.

Looking Glass Library™ is a trademark and logo of Magic Wagon.

Printed in the United States.

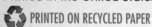 PRINTED ON RECYCLED PAPER

Text by Mari Kesselring
Illustrations by Ronnie Rooney
Edited by Holly Saari
Interior layout and design by Emily Love
Cover design by Emily Love

Library of Congress Cataloging-in-Publication Data

Kesselring, Mari.
  October / by Mari Kesselring ; illustrated by Ronnie Rooney ; content consultant, Susan Kesselring.
    p. cm. — (Months of the year)
  ISBN 978-1-60270-637-8
  1. October—Juvenile literature. 2. Calendar—Juvenile literature. I. Rooney, Ronnie, ill. II. Kesselring, Susan. III. Title.
  CE13.K485 2010
  398'.33—dc22
                          2008050700

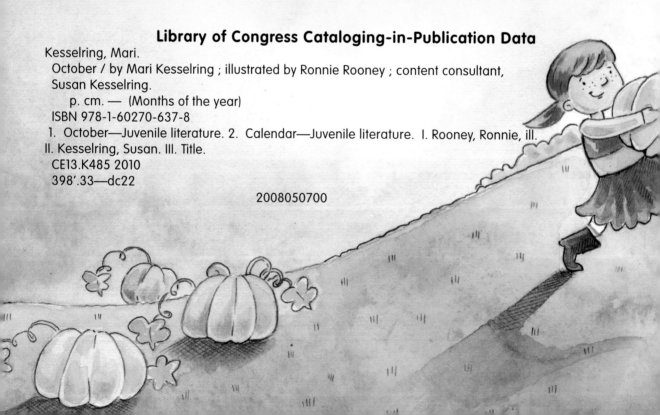

What is the month
that comes after September?
It starts with an *O*.
Do you remember?

It is October!

Is that what you said?

Let's get some October

facts in your head.

5

October is month number ten.
That's so great!
Many years ago, it
was month number eight.

In October,
leaves fall off the trees.
Try to catch them
as they float on the breeze.

8

Yom Kippur is the name
of one special day.
People who are Jewish
fast and pray.

This month has
Columbus Day.
Christopher Columbus
sailed a long way!

October has a
fire safety week.
Gather around.
Listen to a firefighter speak.

Pop! Pop! Pop!

What is that noise?

It's Popcorn Poppin' Month
for girls and boys.

Can you give
a great big roar?
October celebrates
the dinosaur!

The last day in this month
is day 31.
It's Halloween.
Time for some dress up fun!

October is over!

What will we do?

Who is ready for November?

I am. Are you?

Fire Safety

Talk to your parents about fire safety. Your family can make a plan for what to do if there is a fire. It is great to practice fire safety!

Paper Jack-o'-Lantern

Halloween is in October. You can make your own paper jack-o'-lantern. Cut out an orange circle. Cut out a nose, eyes, and a mouth in that circle. Then, glue the orange circle to a yellow piece of paper. See your paper jack-o'-lantern glow!

Words to Know

celebrate—to enjoy something, such as a holiday.
fast—to give up eating food for a religious holiday.
November—the eleventh month of the year. It comes after October.
pray—to communicate with God.
September—the ninth month of the year. It comes after August.

Web Sites

To learn more about October, visit ABDO Group online at **www.abdopublishing.com**. Web sites about October are featured on our Book Links page. These links are routinely monitored and updated to provide the most current information available.